To Thomas.
Love
uncle John.
may 7th. 1998.

THE COMPLETE CANDLEMAKER

THE COMPLETE CANDLEMAKER
Ann Hirst-Smith

Photographs and drawings by
Peter Hirst-Smith

VNR VAN NOSTRAND REINHOLD COMPANY
NEW YORK CINCINNATI TORONTO LONDON MELBOURNE

For my mother

Author: Ann Hirst-Smith   Title: The Complete Candlemaker
Code Number: G 3414–000–7

Van Nostrand Reinhold Company Regional Offices:
New York   Cincinnati   Chicago   Millbrae   Dallas
Van Nostrand Reinhold Company International Offices:
London   Toronto   Melbourne

Printed in Great Britain
Published in the United States of America in 1974 by
Van Nostrand Reinhold Company
A Division of Litton Educational Publishing Inc.
450 West 33rd Street, New York, N. Y. 10001

16 15 14 13 12 11 10 9 8 7 6 5 4 3 2 1

Library of Congress Cataloging in Publication Data
Hirst-Smith, Ann.
        The complete candlemaker.

        Bibliograpy: p.
        1. Candlemaking. I. Title.
TT896.5.H57   745.59′3   74-7823
ISBN 0-442-23414-7 (cloth)
ISBN 0-442-23413-9 (pbk.)

Contents

Introduction

The down-to-earth combination of wax and wick offers a surprisingly wide range of creative possibilities. To make a candle that burns perfectly and looks good, you need only follow a few basic rules. But they are only a starting point: they open the door to endless experiments with shape, colour, and texture. If the experiment fails, the materials can nearly always be rescued. If it succeeds, your candle is not only good to look at: it is also useful.

The Complete Candlemaker isn't written for the person who wants a 'recipe' for every candle he makes. While all the technical information I have found necessary in my own candlemaking experience is included, and many specific projects are detailed, my aim has been to encourage a creative, exploratory approach to an age-old craft.

I hope that *The Complete Candlemaker* will show that the only limitations on the scope of your own candlemaking are your own imagination and capacity for invention.

How to use this book

Although you may be tempted to wade straight in to the candle projects, please read the chapters that precede the projects first. They will help you to understand the materials you are using, and to take the correct safety precautions. Later chapters explain how to cope with the basic techniques of making moulded candles, and provide a useful reference source for the novice candlemaker.

In the main section of the book, the candle projects themselves introduce many different techniques using the equipment you have to hand, and show the sheer variety that candlemaking offers. Decorating your candle can often offer the solution to a ruined finish on a moulded candle – and can transform even the plainest object into something really attractive; and I have outlined all the basic techniques so that you can apply them as you wish to your own candles. If you get really hooked on candle-making, you'll want to extend your range of equipment and tools, so a later section makes some suggestions both for ready-made and make-it-yourself tools that will help you achieve different finishes.

Safety first

It cannot be stressed too often that the materials used in making candles are potentially dangerous. Wax (and particularly paraffin wax) catches fire easily, and can cause very serious burns. For this reason, candlemaking is not a suitable activity for children.

Protect your working area

1   Wherever you choose to work, you should make certain that all surfaces which you, or your materials, will contact are adequately protected. Scraping wax off linoleum or a kitchen working surface is a tedious task – and often, if the wax has been dyed, leaves an ineradicable stain.

2   Even if you have your own workroom, never allow deposits of wax to build up on any surface – they constitute a fire risk. Cover ALL surfaces generously with newspaper: it will make life easier in the long run.

3   If you spill some molten wax, wipe it up as quickly as possible with a rag or kitchen paper. Make sure that your waste bin is well away from any source of heat or flame, and empty it regularly.

4   If you are working in the kitchen, protect the top of your cooker with a 'jacket' of aluminium foil, cut or torn to fit snugly around the burners. This will prevent damage to the surface of the cooker, and you won't have to embark on a long cleaning job after every candlemaking session – simply lift off the foil.

5   It's very easy to drip wax on a lighted burner. To be absolutely safe, always use an asbestos mat, whether you cook with gas or electricity.

6   Finally, never leave your heat source switched on when you're not using it.

Protect yourself

1   Wax is as lethal to your clothing as it is to your work surface. It's often impossible to remove wax dye stains, and the wax itself will only dissolve in pretty hot water. It makes sense, therefore, to wear an overall and old shoes.

2   Some candlemaking techniques involve pouring wax at extremely high temperatures. Try to wear gloves, or cover your hand in a cloth, for this sort of activity. It's easy enough to spill a few drops of wax.

3   Never stand too close to a container full of molten wax. If it gets spilt, you'll get burned.

In case of emergency . . .

If you have taken all the precautions listed above, you should have minimized the fire risk. However, if a fire does occur, throw a cloth over the flames (NOT one which has been used for mopping up spilt wax), or use a foam extinguisher, and remove all inflammable materials from the area.

NEVER try pouring wax which has caught fire down the sink: it will splutter and may burn you. And you will almost certainly block your drain.

If you spill wax on your skin, let it harden (a little cold water run on to it helps), and then peel it off. Serious burns should have the immediate attention of a doctor.

Materials

Wax

Pure wax is a mixture of fatty acids and alcohol, is expensive, hard to come by, and difficult to use in moulds since its melting temperature can be very high indeed and it does not contract sufficiently in cooling to release your finished candle from the sides of the mould. Candlemakers use pure waxes, therefore, primarily as hardening additives, but they are not in any way necessary, and the only pure wax you are likely to encounter is beeswax. Beeswax, and the 'standard' candlemaking material, paraffin wax, are the two types of wax with which we are concerned in this book. Both are relatively inexpensive and readily available from your candlemakers' supplier.

Paraffin wax

Paraffin wax is basically a simple petroleum by-product, but don't be tempted, if the opportunity presents itself, to buy directly from the manufacturer of petroleum by-

Fig. 1 Two of the ways in which you can buy paraffin wax: block and granular.

products. The paraffin wax sold by candlemakers' suppliers is specially formulated, refined, and normally has a controlled melting point of between 143° and 150°F (62° and 65°C) although wax with a lower melting point is also available.

You can buy paraffin wax from your supplier in solid slabs or in bags of flakes. Either way it is sold by the pound.

Paraffin wax is fairly hard, and gives a smooth-burning candle. Its melting point makes it suitable for use in pretty well any kind of mould – a high melting point might buckle, for instance, a plastic mould – and the ideal temperature for pouring is between 180° and 200°F (82° and 93°C). It is important to remember this, as pouring at a lower or a higher temperature might impair the surface and burning qualities of the finished candle.

If you buy paraffin wax in block or slab form, you will probably want to break it up into more manageable chunks. Rather than hammer it direct, it's easier, and less messy, to put your block inside an old pillowcase before applying the hammer to it.

Beeswax

Beeswax is, as I have said, a pure wax, and does not produce a perfect candle when used on its own as a moulding wax. As a paraffin wax additive, however, it gives a candle a smoother, creamier finish, and imparts a delicious honey smell to the candle when it burns. Used in its natural colour (the pale golden glow of honeycomb), in a fairly generous proportion with uncoloured paraffin wax, it imparts its own colour – but may cause you difficulty when you try to remove your candle from the mould. Further, adding a small percentage of beeswax to paraffin wax helps to make a candle burn more slowly, and minimizes dripping.

Beeswax is sold in sheets, either plain or 'honeycombed', by your supplier, both in its natural colour or ready-dyed in a variety of subtle shades. Beeswax sheets are the basis of some of the easiest candles of all to make (no moulds, and no melting is required), and are excellent for appliqué work. Small discs of beeswax, for use as a paraffin wax additive, may also be bought.

11

Stearin

Stearin, made from a mixture of animal and vegetable fats, is an invaluable aid to the candlemaker. A white, flaky substance, which you should melt separately and then add to your melted paraffin wax, it gives your candle a harder finish (hot summer days can sometimes cause a pure paraffin wax candle to bend), prevents the candle from guttering, and greatly improves mould release. Mixed as it melts with wax dye, it gives a more brilliant colour to the finished candle.

Stearin is purchased by weight from your supplier. There is no absolute formula for the amount of stearin you should add to paraffin wax, but I find a ratio of 90% paraffin wax, or paraffin wax and beeswax, to 10% stearin excellent for most purposes.

Fig. 2 Stearin, sometimes called stearic acid or sterene, is bought by weight in flakes or, in this case, granules.

Wicks

A candle burns because melted wax travels up a wick to 'feed' the flame with vapour, which keeps the candle alight. If your wick is too narrow, it will be unable to relay a sufficient supply of molten wax to the flame, and the candle will extinguish itself. Conversely, if the wick is too large, the heat from the large flame will melt too wide a surface area of the candle, creating a 'pond' into which the wick will finally collapse – and extinguish itself. Obtaining a perfect relationship between the size – particularly the diameter – of a candle and the size of the wick is essential for smooth, continuous burning.

A piece of ordinary string inserted into the centre of a candle is no use as a wick: it lacks the properties to conduct the molten wax up to the flame. To make your own wicks with ordinary white string, you must braid the string firmly, using two, three, or more strands according to the size of wicking you want. (It is often difficult to gauge this in advance, particularly if you are a beginner at wick-making.) Then soak the braided string in a solution of one cup of water, two tablespoonfuls of borax, and one table-spoonful of salt for six hours or so, and hang it up to dry thoroughly. The wick is now ready to use.

Making your own wicks, however, is hardly necessary today, when commercially-made wicking is available very cheaply indeed. Furthermore, it comes labelled according to the diameter of the candle you propose to make, from ½in. (13mm.) up to around 4in (100mm.). If your supplier does not label his wicking in this way, ask his advice. In any case, it is sensible to keep a good stock of wicking in all sizes.

It is often a help to dip the wicking in molten wax and leave it to set before inserting it in a mould since it is easier to guide and control a rigid wick than a floppy one. In the USA, metal-core wicking (unavailable in Britain) is available from your supplier. There is no need to pre-wax it as a fine thread of lead or magnesium runs through the centre of the wicking, making it rigid. When using metal-core wicking, you may find it difficult to light a finished candle for the first time, but pre-waxing just the tip of the wick often helps.

13

Sometimes the mould you choose will not have a hole in its base through which you can anchor the wick before pouring in the molten wax. In this case, buy a wick retainer – a metal disc to which you attach the wick – from your supplier. This is simply lowered by the wick into the centre of the mould base.

Wax dyes

It is essential to use a wax-based dye to colour wax: nothing else will work. Providing they are pure wax without plastic additives, ordinary crayons are fine if you have nothing else available, though they may spoil the burning quality of the finished candle. For the best results – and much more cheaply – you should use commercial wax dyes. These are available in liquid, powder, and block form.

Block dyes are best for larger quantities of wax. Each block of dye has been formulated to colour a certain number of pounds of wax (check the dye label – the amount varies with the maker). Mixing commercial shades to get subtler tones isn't easy with block dyes unless you are prepared to mix large quantities – cutting the blocks is awkward.

Liquid and powder dyes, however, can be used in minute quantities, and give much more freedom to the candle-maker who wants to make a batch of candles all in different colours. Add the liquid or powder very sparingly, little by little, to the molten wax: these dyes are highly concentrated, and molten wax, being transparent, gives a false impression of colour intensity to the inexperienced candlemaker. With practice, you will come to know how much dye to use, but a beginner, or anyone trying out a new shade, can effectively

Fig. 3 You can use any of several types of dye for colouring candlemaking wax: wax crayons, liquid dye, powder dye, or dye discs.

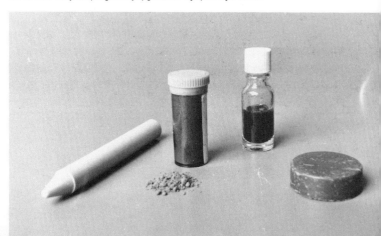

use a simple colour test. Trickle a little of the dyed, melted wax on to a non-porous white surface (a plate or a piece of plastic laminate are fine), and let it set. You will see the colour change as the wax becomes opaque. Remember, though, that the colour will be many times denser in the finished candle, and *don't* continue adding more dye till the test trickle looks exactly like the colour you want.

You can create exciting tones and colours by mixing dyes (the colour chart on page 38 will help you to do this successfully). Left-over blocks of dyed wax and unsuccessful dyed candles can be melted down together to create a new shade, or redyed for the same purpose; but remember that tipping multi-coloured leftovers into the pot will produce a candle that is simply a revolting muddy brown.

Dye should be added when the wax is melted, and, if added to the separately melting stearin, will give a clearer, more brilliant colour.

Perfumes

It is a complete waste of time to tip a few generous drops of your favourite French scent into melted wax. Just as wax-based dye is necessary for candlemaking, so oil-based perfumes are the only ones which will combine successfully with wax.

Wax perfumes are available from your supplier (who may sometimes also stock pre-scented wax). They are highly concentrated, and a little goes a long way. Nobody enjoys burning a candle that constantly emits an overpowering scent. You can add a few drops of perfume to the melted wax just before pouring – this scents the entire candle; or, when you have poured the wax into the mould and it is beginning to harden, punch a few holes with a long skewer around the wick, and pour a drop of perfume into each. This gives a less even result, but it is especially useful for large candles, where, in time, you may wish to re-melt and re-use the outer shell once the candle is burned down.

Personally, I find wax perfumes heavy, and I use them sparingly. If you are going to perfume a candle, bear in mind the time of year, the shape and colour of the candle, and scent it accordingly. A large black obelisk, for example, would seem odd if it were floral-scented!

Basic technique

The workroom

For most people, the kitchen will be the only workroom available for their candlemaking activities. Actually, apart from the fact that it has to be prepared and cleaned up again after every candlemaking session, the kitchen is ideal. It contains, after all, pretty well every essential in the way of equipment: a source of heat (the cooker), running water, plenty of work surfaces, and an endless range of pots, pans, moulds, and other equipment which can readily be brought into service.

If you plan to work in the kitchen, begin by closing all cupboard doors and make sure you cover any exposed food. Wax dye – particularly the powdered variety – floats in the air, and will stain anything it comes into contact with.

Prepare yourself and your work surfaces as described in the chapter on safety (page 8), assemble your equipment, and you're ready to go.

If, on the other hand, you are lucky enough to have your own candlemaking workroom, it will need to have some heat source for melting the wax. If you can't manage a radiant electric ring or two, or the equivalent gas burners, a straightforward camping stove or Calor gas stove is fine, providing it is anchored for safety to the work surface. Running water – hot and cold – is a help, although you can get by with jugs and buckets. You'll want plenty of bench space and storage space for your equipment and your finished candles. You may want to explore the possibilities of using electric tools to help you in your candle-making, so three or four extra electric points at work level (well away from the water and heat sources) will be useful.

Equipment

If you are the possessor of a kitchen with a cooker and running water, you have at your fingertips all the essential equipment for candlemaking.

Start with two old saucepans, one large enough to hold the other. The larger, filled with water and placed on a gas ring or electric burner, will provide adequate conditions for melting your wax in the smaller saucepan, carefully lowered into the hot water. Additionally, you will need a sugar thermometer (to gauge the temperature of the melted wax), a pair of scissors (to cut and trim wicks), and some Plasticine or mould seal from your supplier.

Ambitious candlemakers can extend their equipment as they gain confidence and develop new techniques. Larger melting containers (metal buckets etc.), and metal jugs and ladles with lips for easier pouring of melted wax are invaluable investments. If you can pick up an old electric clothes boiler from your junk shop, you will have a marvellous method of melting large quantities of wax at a controlled temperature – and permanent storage for it, too.

I find a craft knife almost an essential – and a butane blowtorch, which is invaluable for wax welding jobs, creating unusual finishes, and 'tidying up' candles with a damaged surface.

For more ideas, see the section on advanced equipment (page 114).

Choosing and preparing a mould

Pretty well any container, *provided it is clean and the open top is at least as wide as the base*, will convert almost instantly into a candle mould.

Home-made paper moulds are easy to make if you are good with a pair of scissors. Once you have prepared the basic shape, reinforce it with struts or sheets of wood or cardboard, and seal the corners with masking tape, as shown. Make a base (a paper-covered piece of wood or cardboard), and make a hole in the centre for the wick. Seal the base to the sides with masking tape. Finally, strengthen the top of the mould with masking tape, making a cross diagonally from corner to corner. The centre of this cross can be used to hold the wick in place. Prepare the inner surface of the mould with a thin, even layer of kitchen oil or special silicone mould spray (from your supplier).

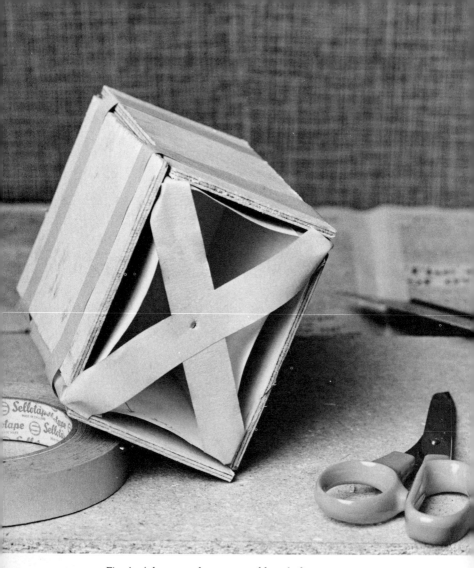

Fig. 4 A home-made paper mould ready for use.

Any kind of paper will do, but aluminium foil or grease-proof paper are best.

Milk cartons and yoghourt pots and most kinds of disposable container can be pressed into service as moulds. Waxed paper cartons will probably need to be strutted in the same way as ordinary paper cartons, and strengthened all round with a layer of masking tape, and you should apply the same procedure to thin plastic containers which might melt when you pour in hot wax. Make a hole in the base of the container for the wick, and, if you want a smooth finish and are thinking of using the container again as a mould, coat the inner surface with oil or silicone spray. Unfortun-

18

ately, even these precautions may not guarantee that you can save the container after use: resign yourself to the possibility of having to tear the mould away to release the candle.

Plastic and copper piping, such as plumbers use, make excellent moulds: buy off-cuts from a local builders' merchant, and saw off the length of piping you require. Make certain that, standing on end, it is completely vertical (use a plumb line or a spirit level balanced on a sheet of card or wood to check this), and finish off the sawn edges very carefully with fine sandpaper or an electric sander. Make sure there are no internal protrusions which could hinder mould release or spoil the surface of your candle. If you like, you can make a couple of notches in

Fig. 5 Plastic rainwater piping ready for use. Note the careful sealing of the tin lid which acts as a base.

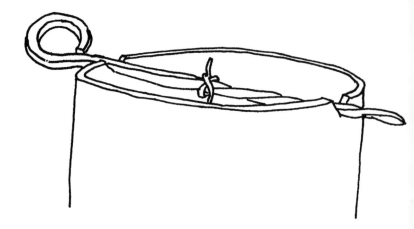

Fig. 6 Notches made in the top of a length of plastic piping make it easier for you to keep the wick, safely anchored to a skewer or pencil with a knot, absolutely central.

one end of the mould, to hold a pencil or skewer from which you can suspend the wick. Make a base of paper, card, plastic, or metal – or simply use a lid from a bottle or jar which will accommodate the base of the candle. Make a hole in the centre for the wick, and seal the base to the body of the mould with Plasticine, mould seal or putty.

Household crockery provides a vast storehouse of mould possibilities. Cups, straight-sided jugs, mugs, and vases make excellent moulds – as long as you are careful that the shape of your chosen container will allow you to extract the finished candle without breaking the mould. If in doubt, test the container first by oiling it and then pressing in sufficient Plasticine to fill it. Turn it upside down. If the Plasticine 'candle' releases itself, you're OK. This, incidentally, is also an excellent way of finding out what a candle made in a crockery mould will look like. Obviously, drilling a wick hole in the base of a piece of crockery is impractical, so either use a wick retainer or when you make candles by this method you must insert the wick after the candle has set. Try to use wide, large containers: a tall, narrow candle will split if you try to insert a wick in it once it has set.

Jelly moulds are fun to try as candle moulds, and animal shapes make attractive children's candles. If you buy a mould specially for candlemaking, drill a hole for the wick at a suitable point. If you're using one of your everyday kitchen moulds, use a wick retainer if you can fit it into the mould – or be prepared to insert the wick after the candle has set. Oil the mould before use, and, if you propose to use it again for jelly-making, boil it afterwards.

Commercial rubber, plastic, glass and metal moulds can be bought in all shapes and sizes from your supplier. All *you* have to do is make sure the mould is clean before use. It is advisable to use a silicone spray on rubber moulds, especially where the candle design embodies a lot of detail and nooks and crannies. A really well sprayed mould interior will help the wax to penetrate every corner.

Do-it-yourself rubber and plaster of Paris moulds are useful if you have an object whose shape you think would make

Fig. 7 A selection of home-made, ready-made, and commercial moulds to start you thinking.

an attractive candle. Simply take a cast of the object following the instructions that come with the plaster or the moulding rubber, and prepare the mould as you would any other.

Tin cans are usually more trouble than they're worth. All have a seam running down the inside, where the can has been welded, and unless you plan to decorate the final candle to disguise the indentation this will leave, you should give tin cans a miss. Remember too, that at each end of a can, just beneath the lid, is a metal lip. Either remove this with a special can opener when you remove the lid, or bend the lip outwards with metal cutters.

Fig. 8   Tin cans pose problems of their own: note the lip inside the upper rim (cut it off or bend it back), and the seam running down the side.

General hints

Candles with a smooth, shiny surface are the result of really clean moulds. Make sure there is no dust or old wax adhering to the interior: most moulds, with care, can be washed, and then thoroughly dried. Petroleum lighter fuel will clean metal moulds beautifully. Secondly, always store moulds where they can't collect dirt or dust – in plastic bags or in a cupboard. Metal moulds, which might rust if left for long periods, can be coated with oil or sprayed with silicone spray or wax silicone furniture polish.

Although oiling the mould helps both mould release and candle finish, it is only really necessary when you are using an un-waxed paper mould. Don't ever apply a thick layer of oil that will run inside the mould, and may finally damage the shape of the finished candle: a whisk over with a fine paint-brush or a cotton wool swab is all that is necessary. Silicone mould spray is, of course, better than oil.

Some moulds may need support when you are using them: rubber moulds and jelly moulds are good examples. Your supplier will have ready-made stands for commercial rubber moulds, but you can always build your own support frame from which you can suspend them – or bury them carefully in a box of sand or salt, making certain that the wick hole in the mould is thoroughly sealed and the top surface completely covered to keep out stray sand or salt granules which might damage the candle.

Inserting the wick

1 Before pouring the wax

Your mould may have a hole in the centre of the base through which you can thread your wick. If this is the case, take a length of wicking slightly longer than the height of the mould, and tie a simple knot in one end. Dip the length of wicking in molten wax – preferably colourless or the colour you propose to make your finished candle – and hang it up to dry. Insert the unknotted end of the wick through the hole in the base, and pull the wick taut, so that the knot is tight against the outer mould base. Seal the knot carefully to the mould to avoid the melted wax leaking, using Plasticine or mould seal. If you are using a

23

commercial mould, it may well have a raised base – so that, even when the knot has been sealed, the mould will still stand upright. If you are using a home-made mould, you won't have a raised base, and you won't be able to stand your mould upright. A simple, makeshift platform of two blocks of wood, two foil-covered books, or any two objects of exactly the same height, is fine: simply balance the mould between them. Alternatively, you can bury the mould in a sand- or salt-pit.

Twist the loose end of the wick round a pencil or skewer, and tie a knot if necessary, first making sure that the wick is absolutely vertical to your working bench, and absolutely centred at the *top* of the mould. Alternatively, make

Fig. 9 A commercial mould ready for use. The wick is knotted and sealed at the base, and secured around a skewer at the top with another knot.

a criss-cross on the top of the mould with masking tape, and catch the loose end of the wick into the centre of the cross. If you decide on this method, take care, when pouring, not to pour hot wax on to the tape: it could release the wick.

If you are using a mould without a wick hole (for example, a piece of household crockery), use (if you have one) a special wick retainer. Simply anchor the wick to the metal retaining disc, and lower it carefully into the centre of the mould. Fix as before at the top surface of the mould.

2 After the candle is set

If a wick retainer is neither to hand nor suitable for the mould you are using, you will have to insert the wick after the candle has set hard. To do this, remove the candle from its mould, mark the centre with a skewer, and begin to bore a hole vertically through the mark you have made. You can do this with a narrow-gauge hand drill, an electric drill (at a fairly slow speed), a soldering iron, or simply with an ordinary kitchen skewer or knitting needle.

Drilling needs care: do it in short bursts, cleaning out the hole regularly to ensure that the drill can bore downwards without exerting pressure on the candle itself that will cause it to split. For long candles, you will need an extra long drill bit. See page 115 for making your own.

Using a hot soldering iron or a heated skewer or knitting needle is a slower, but less hazardous method. You'll have to build your own special attachment for a soldering iron to achieve sufficient length (see page 114), but a skewer, held over a flame for a few moments, and then applied vertically to the surface of the candle, is an excellent alternative. Just keep heating, and then probing gently.

Once you have made a channel through the entire length of the candle, you can insert the wick. Again, it's easier to manoeuvre a wick that has been pre-waxed. Tie a knot at one end of the wick, and push it through from the base until it emerges at the top surface. Stand the candle on its top surface, exposing the base, and 'top up' the base with a little molten wax specially reserved for the purpose, to secure, and conceal, the knotted end of the wick. Alternatively, melt the inner surface of the base with a blowtorch

Fig. 10 If you have inserted the wick *after* pouring, as in the case of this sand candle, you will have to 'tidy up' the upper surface, because you will almost certainly have made an ugly hole in the centre of the candle.

until it has caught in the wick. Leave until the wax has set Turn the candle the right way up: you will find that boring the wick hole has left the top surface of the candle some-what untidy. If you have a blowtorch, this is when it can be indispensable. Working with a very low flame, and taking great care, soften up the surface area of the candle so that wax melts and runs down the central wick shaft. Work only around the centre of the candle, to avoid caus-ing dripping round the sides. When you are satisfied that the surface is completely smooth and the wick securely anchored, leave it to harden.

If you don't have a blowtorch, top up the wick shaft with an eye dropper full of liquid wax, and polish the top surface of the candle with an old but clean nylon stocking to give it a shiny finish.

Finally, trim the wick to about a quarter of an inch (6 mm.) above the surface of the candle.

If you can lay your hands on a large darning needle, a kitchen larding needle, or a special wicking needle (from your supplier), you will make the job of wick insertion a lot easier. The wick often gets 'lost' round about the middle of the candle.

Setting a candle

Once your wax has been poured into the mould, you can go away and leave it to set – which could be up to twenty-four

Fig. 11 A commercial wicking needle. You can, of course, improvise your own out of a length of wire, looped at one end.

hours depending on the size of the candle – or you can 'help it along', and achieve variants of finish, by doing different things with it.

For example, leave the candle for half a minute or so after the wax has been poured, to allow any air bubbles to rise to the surface. Then carefully lift your mould, and place it in a bath of cold water, filled to exactly the height of the mould. If possible, cover your mould before placing it in the bath (which could be a large jug, a plastic bucket or basin, or simply your sink or bath). You might have to weight the top of the mould to keep it standing up – so try to use a mould with a level top (i.e. with the wick secured either in notches in the side of the mould, or with masking tape). Any object that will balance on top of the mould without toppling it will do as a weight. Leave the candle until it is set, which should take three to four hours depending on the size of the candle. This method gives a smooth, bubble-free surface, and provides the absolutely correct temperature for perfect wax contraction and setting. Obviously, you can't use it for unwaxed paper moulds, and you would have to rig up some kind of waterproof support frame for rubber moulds and jelly moulds.

Fig. 12 A cooling bath. It's important that the level of water in the bath is exactly the same as the level of wax in the mould.

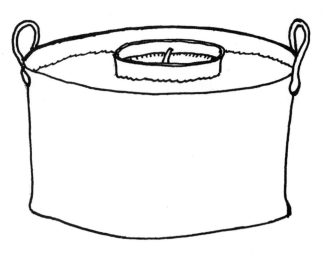

Fig. 13 As a candle sets, the wax contracts, leaving a deep hollow well in the centre.

Alternatively, leave the candle for half a minute or so, and then put it straight into the fridge or freezer. Your finished candle will very likely have lots of tiny surface cracks (known as 'thermal cracking'), and may have an interesting mottled texture.

29

'Topping up'

As it solidifies, wax contracts, and thus as a candle sets, a 'well' appears in the centre of the top surface. This has to be filled up, and you should always reserve sufficient wax from the batch you prepare for your candle to allow for this. Ideally, watch the surface of your candle for the moment it begins to show any hollowing. Then make a few holes in this to break the surface tension. As the candle becomes firmer, prod more holes, and pour in a little wax to level up the surface. *Never pour more wax than is necessary to fill up the holes in the candle*, or you will cause a layering or ridging of the finished candle, and ruin the

Fig. 14 The correct 'topping up' procedure entails piercing a number of small holes in the skin of the candle as the well forms, and then pouring in more melted wax at the right temperature.

candle's finish. It may be necessary to make the surface holes three times before the candle's surface solidifies without contracting in the centre to form a well. It is worthwhile doing this, however, as it ensures that the finished candle will burn smoothly, and without guttering or spitting, right to the end.

If you *must* take half-measures for some reason or another, leave the candle until it is set, but still warm and not ready to be unmoulded. Then top it up in one go.

Making a simple moulded candle step by step

1   Prepare your working area with newspaper, making sure it's not put near a naked flame. Put on an overall.

2   Assemble your moulds, wicking, and sealing medium (Plasticine) on your work surface.

3   Make sure your moulds are clean. Wipe them out with kitchen paper or a dry cloth to make absolutely certain.

4   If you are using block paraffin wax, place a block inside an old pillow case or large plastic bag, and break it up into conveniently-sized pieces with a hammer.

5   Take a large saucepan or other suitable container, and fill one quarter full with water. Place over a lighted gas ring or electric radiant ring, and bring water to the boil.

6   Place the desired quantity of solid or granulated paraffin wax into a container which will stand in the saucepan of water, and gently lower the smaller container into the water, being careful not to let any get in with the wax.

7   Turn the heat down below the water, so that it just simmers gently, and leave the wax to melt.

8   Cut off suitable lengths of wicking, knot each at one end, and dip them into the container of melting wax. Hang them up to dry.

9   Insert the wicks in the base of the mould, pulling them through until the knot is tight against the base. Knot carefully and seal the wick hole.

10   Stand your moulds upright – on platforms if necessary.

11   Now centre the wick at the top of the mould, and fix it – either at the centre of a criss-cross of masking tape, or by

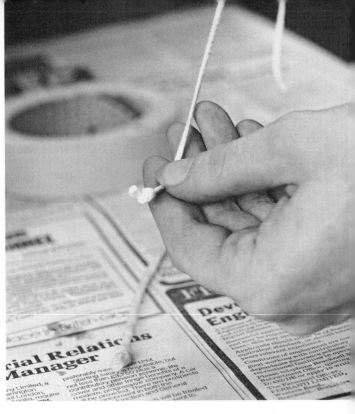

Fig. 15   When you have chosen your mould, cut off a suitable length of wicking, knot it at one end, and then dip it . . .

Fig. 16   . . . into hot wax. Leave to dry.

Fig. 17 Insert the wick at the base of the mould, and pull it through, until the knot is tight against the base.

tying or taping it round a skewer or pencil placed across the top of the mould.

12 Make absolutely certain that the wick is taut and central.

13 When the paraffin wax has melted, you can transfer some of it to other containers if you wish to make a batch of candles in different colours, or if you do not wish to dye the entire quantity.

Fig. 18 Pour in melted wax at the correct temperature, aiming for the centre of the mould, and trying not to pour down the edge.

14 Now is the time to add beeswax to your melted paraffin wax if you wish to. Slide it into the wax container gently, and leave it to melt.

15 Add stearin, spooning it carefully into the melted wax; and immediately add wax dye if your candles are to be coloured. Stir in the wax and stearin with a clean, dry metal spoon.

34

16   If you have dyed the wax, and wish to test the colour, wait for the stearin to dissolve, and then apply the simple test on page 15.

17   Slide your sugar thermometer into the container full of wax, and watch for the temperature to rise up to 180° F (82° C). When it does so, be ready to remove the container of wax from the heat source.

18   Carefully pour the wax into the mould, using either a pre-heated metal jug or a spoon (a soup ladle is ideal). Aim your pouring at the centre of the mould, trying not to let drips of wax form on the inner surfaces.

Fig. 19   The wax will now be left to cool, or the mould inserted in a cooling bath.

Fig. 20 Shake the candle gently out of its mould once it has set. If you don't hold the candle as it comes out of the mould, disaster might well follow!

19 Remember to save enough wax to 'top up'.

20 Turn off the heat source, and set your candle in any of the ways described on page 28.

21 While your candle is setting, 'top up' in the ways described on page 30.

22 Your candle is set when it seems to have shrunk from the sides of the mould. When this has happened, remove

the tape or skewer restraining the wick, and turn the mould upside down, cupping your hand over the open end of the mould. Remove the seal around the knot of wicking, and either untie the knot and straighten out the wick, or cut it off with a craft knife.

23 Now shake the candle gently out of the mould, holding the candle itself very loosely, so as not to damage the surface.

24 Stand the candle up, and, if necessary, trim the wick to about a quarter of an inch (6 mm.) above the surface. Your candle is now ready to light.

Fig. 21 The finished candle.

For reference

Wax

2 lb. (0·9 kg.) of solid paraffin wax = 2 pints (1·14 litres) of liquid wax.

Paraffin wax should be poured at between 180° and 200° F (82° to 93° C). It melts at between 143° and 150° F (61° and 65° C).

Beeswax melts at approximately 145° F (63° C).

A good ratio of stearin additive to wax is 1 : 10.

Colour mixing

1 part red + 1 part yellow + 1 part blue = BLACK
6 parts white + 1 part red   = PINK
5 parts orange + 1 part black   = BROWN
1 part red + 1 part yellow   = ORANGE
1 part red + 1 part blue   = PURPLE
2 parts pink + 1 part blue   = LAVENDER
1 part blue + 1 part yellow   = GREEN
3 parts green + 1 part red   = MOSS GREEN

Candlemaking projects

Here are twenty-four ways to use the basic knowledge and technique you have now gained. Each is different, and every single project could be the starting point for experiments of your own.

A simple rolled beeswax candle

Equipment

Sheet of beeswax
Length of wicking

Method Soften the sheet of beeswax in front of a radiator for a few moments until it is pliable, and then lay it on a flat surface. Lay a length of wick along one edge of the sheet

Fig. 22 Before you begin rolling a beeswax candle, anchor the wick firmly by turning over the edge of the beeswax sheet.

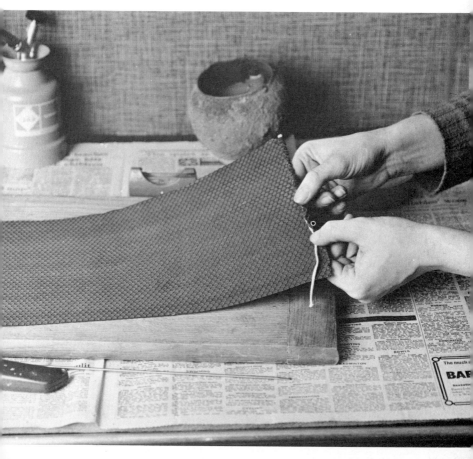

so that it protrudes about a quarter of an inch (6 mm.) at one end. Fold the edge of the beeswax sheet over the wick, so that it is evenly held. Trying to keep the fold absolutely straight, now gently but firmly roll the beeswax sheeting up, starting from the edge where the wick is. When you reach the end of the sheet, press the exposed edge gently down so that it seals itself to the rest of the sheet. Turn in the base of the candle slightly if the candle is tall and thin, as this will prevent damage to the base when you insert the candle in a candlestick.

Variations   Use more than one sheet of beeswax, butting each carefully up against each other as you roll (remember to use a larger wick the larger the candle is likely to be). Use sheets of different coloured beeswax, finishing with a complete 'circle' of the outside colour.

Fig. 23   Rolling the candle.

Fig. 24 The finished candle.

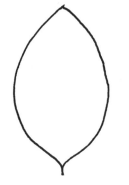

A beeswax rose candle

Equipment

Beeswax sheet
Narrow wicking
Scissors or craft knife

Method Make a small rolled beeswax candle, about the size of a normal bought cake candle, using the same method described on the previous page.

Divide the rest of the beeswax sheet into strips roughly as wide as the rolled beeswax candle, and, using scissors or a craft knife, cut the strips into petal shapes – narrow, slightly pointed ones for the centre of the rose, and flatter, wider ones for the outside petals. Using the candle as the centre of the flower, build up the petals around it, pressing them firmly to the base of

Fig. 25 It's easier to show in a drawing how to build up the petal shapes (here, too, are rough outlines for cutting them).

42

the candle, until your rose is complete. Now bend the petals until they resemble a half-blown rose. Tidy up the base of the rose, and decorate it with tiny green leaves.

Beeswax roses make excellent cake candles, mounted on a foil or non-absorbent paper base (to catch drips). They will burn for about fifteen minutes.

Variations   Try making other kinds of flower. Add 'stems' by attaching a length of rigid wire to the base of the flower, and covering it with beeswax of a suitable colour. At Christmas, make little sprigs of holly: green beeswax 'leaves', with rolled balls of red beeswax to represent the holly berries. Add a small, red, rolled beeswax candle to the centre of the cluster of holly berries to make an attractive Christmas cake decoration.

Fig. 26   This is how your finished rose will look.

A paraffin wax rose candle

Equipment
Paraffin wax
Wicking
Thermostatically controlled electric hotplate or frying pan,
  or a bowl of hot water
Toffee tray or shallow baking tin
Craft knife
Soldering iron

Method Pour a layer of paraffin wax about an eighth of
an inch (3 mm.) thick into a toffee tray, and before it has
hardened, cut out petal shapes with your craft knife as
for the beeswax rose, as well as a strip of wax from which
to roll your central candle. Keep the wax strip and the pre-
cut petals soft by placing them in a bowl of hot water, or
on a sheet of foil placed on a hotplate or electric frying pan.
Now build up the flower shape using the tiny candle as the
centre, and bonding each petal with a soldering iron.

A beeswax cube candle

Equipment
Beeswax sheeting
Wicking
Craft knife

Method Decide on the size of candle you want to make,
and cut sheets of beeswax into squares of this size. Use
your craft knife, and measure exactly. Whether your
candle is to be striped (using different coloured sheets of
beeswax) or a single colour, build up two identical heaps of
beeswax squares, laying each square exactly on top of its
predecessor, and pressing gently and evenly to bond the
squares together. When you have achieved the two halves
of your cube, lay the wick along the centre of one half of
the cube, and press it gently in to secure it. Finally, press
the other half of the cube over the wick and then press the
whole candle together to bond the layers securely (using a
book as a press, or a flat piece of wood, is more satisfactory
than pressing with the palm of the hand).

Variations Face the sides and top surface of the candle
with another layer of wax, which can then be carved out
in places to expose the original surface.

Fig. 27 A beeswax cube, built up from several layers of multicoloured beeswax sheeting and then faced with another layer of wax.

A free-form wax block candle

Equipment
Block of paraffin wax
Length of wicking
Shallow container of boiling water
Flat baking sheet
Craft knife
Saw or hot-wire cutter

Method Divide your block of paraffin wax into two un-equal pieces, either with a saw or using the hot wire technique suggested on page 115. However, with the former method, you will probably achieve a ragged edge, and the blocks themselves may acquire dents and scratches. To remedy this, place the container of boiling water on the stove, and lay the baking sheet over the top. Leave it for a few minutes until the surface of the baking sheet heats up. Then place a block of wax on the baking sheet, moving it around until the surface in contact with the baking sheet is smooth. Leave the block to harden up again, and repeat the procedure until every surface of both blocks is as smooth as you want it to be.

Now decide how you want your finished candle to look, by standing the blocks together – perhaps one block vertically, and one horizontally. When you have decided, look at the top surface of the 'candle', and decide where the wick should go. Mark this point with a scratch of your craft knife. Now measure and cut off the length of wick you will need, choosing the broadest possible wick to ensure good burning. Then weld the two blocks together by melting the surfaces which will contact each other, laying the wick along one, and holding them firmly together. You have to be pretty quick to do this successfully – the melted wax surface hardens almost immediately you lift it off the heat source: a second pair of hands (and perhaps a second baking sheet over a second frying pan) make it easier for the beginner. Once you are satisfied that the candle is properly welded, leave it for ten minutes to harden, and trim

Fig. 28 A free-form wax block candle. Since it's so large, there are two wicks instead of just one.

the wick. You may need to 'flatten out' the base of the candle on the baking sheet again if your welding was not entirely accurate, and pick off any wax drips that may have collected with your craft knife.

Variations   Use more than two blocks, and more than one wick. Make blocks of coloured wax yourself in square-sided tins and use these instead of ordinary white wax. Use different coloured wax blocks. Face the outer surfaces of the completed candle with beeswax sheeting cut to size and welded to the paraffin wax surface as before. Dip the finished candle, holding it by the wick, into a large container of melted wax at a temperature of about 170° F (77° C), lift it out, let it set, redip, until an even outer colour is achieved. Carve the candle's surface or decorate it.

A free-form foil and ice candle

Equipment
Length of aluminium foil
Some ice cubes
Wax
Wicking

Method   Crumple a piece of aluminium foil, oiled if you don't want any pieces of foil adhering to the surface of the candle, and unoiled if you want to have a few foil 'high-lights' on the finished article. Shape the crumpled foil to your requirements, bearing in mind that you will have to insert the wick after the candle has set. Now place a few chunks of ice in the foil mould, preferably away from the centre of the candle, where the wick will be inserted. Pour and set in the usual way, and then tear off the foil over a

Fig. 29   A free-form foil and ice candle with multiple wicks, to exploit to the full the different surfaces of the candle.

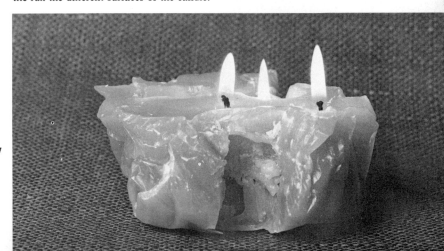

basin. The melted ice leaves holes in the finished candle. Insert the wick.

Variations   Use a small candle (one with a damaged outer surface that wouldn't otherwise be usable is fine) as the centre, as for the ice candle on the next page; make sure your foil 'mould' when filled with wax is the same height as the centre candle.

An ice candle

Equipment
Ready-made, round candle, complete with wick
Wax
Stearin
Cracked ice
Mould the same height as the candle, but at least an inch (25 mm.) wider

Method   Seal the wick hole in the base of your chosen mould, and lower the ready-made candle into the centre. Pour in molten wax of a contrasting colour to that of the candle, to a depth of half an inch (13 mm.), to secure the

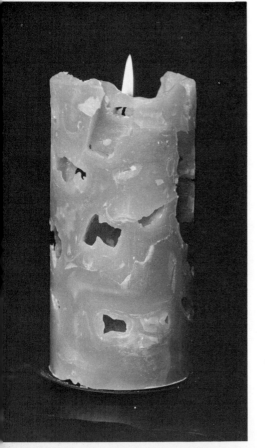

candle in the mould. Leave to set firm. Fill the mould with pieces of ice to within half an inch of the top of the mould, and slowly pour hot wax around the central candle, filling the mould to exactly the top. Leave to set. De-mould over a basin or the sink, as the ice will have melted, then shake the candle vigorously to remove any remaining water.

Variations Soften off the edges of the outer layer with a blowtorch. Dip the whole candle in a hot wax bath.

Fig. 30 An ice candle. Ice candles improve with burning: the lower the central shaft grows, the more interesting the effect of the light glowing through the holes.

48

A sand candle – first method

Equipment
Box of sand
Paraffin wax
Stearin
Wicking
Objects suitable for pressing into the sand to create a
mould

Method   Sift through the sand in the box (which can be
bought in several different colours and consistencies from
your builders' merchant) to separate any lumps, and remove
any stones which might spoil the final finish. Test the
consistency of the sand by taking a handful and pressing it
tightly in the palm of your hand: if it adheres to itself it is
fine. If all the grains remain separate, trickle a little water
into the box and stir it around, but don't add too much as
the dampness of the sand will affect the final finish of the
candle. A fairly dry sand will give a good, thick layer of
wax and sand on the outside of your finished candle; wet
sand will not bond so readily with the hot wax, and will
give a thinner coating of wax and sand on the outside of
the candle.

Once you are happy with the consistency of the sand,
smooth it down so that it is firm, but not tightly packed in

Fig. 31   Making a sand mould by pressing a solid object (in this case half
a talcum powder container) into the sand.

Fig. 32 The finished mould.

its box. Check that the surface is level with a spirit level. Now choose an object whose shape will make a pleasing mould for a candle – half a powder bowl, a flower pot, a mug, a block of wood – and press it (solid side downward if you are using an open-ended object) firmly and evenly into the sand until it has made a deep, well-defined, even impression. Lift out the object carefully, making sure that the impression you have made is not damaged in any way in the process. You may find this difficult at first, but one of the advantages of sand moulds is that you can simply fill in your damaged mould, and start again. Once you are happy with the basic shape, you can embellish it as your fancy dictates. The bowl of a spoon, pressed firmly into the side of your sand mould, will create indentations that, in the finished candle, will appear as bumps. You can give your candle legs by inserting a length of dowelling at a very slight angle into the base of the sand mould in three or four places. Make sure that you insert the length of dowelling to exactly the same depth each time, or your legs will end up with drastically different lengths.

Once you are happy with your mould, heat your wax to at least 180° F (82° C). For this method of candle making

Fig. 33 Pouring the wax into the mould. Take care not to pour down the side of the mould, and thereby spoil the shape.

only, it is permissible (but slightly dangerous) to heat the wax to above 200° F (93° C), since the actual temperature of the wax – as well as the dampness of the sand – affects the thickness of sand and wax: the lower the temperature of the wax, the thinner the sand/wax crust. Choose the pouring temperature you wish. If you want to pour at over 200° F (93° C), wear gloves, and watch the wax carefully as it heats. It will smoke badly. When the correct temperature has been attained, pour the wax smoothly and gently into the very centre of the sand mould, letting not one drop of wax touch the sides, or you will spoil the finish. Fill the mould right to the top: the wax will seethe and bubble in the sand, and the sand will absorb a certain amount of the wax. Now leave the candle (preferably with the sand box covered with a clean sheet of board) until it has set. You will find that you can literally dig out the candle with your hands when the wax has hardened. If the finish is not absolutely perfect (which happens more often than not), carve away at the crust on the outside of the candle until you are happy with it. Slight imperfections can be tackled with emery paper, and a smoother finish can be obtained by going over the entire outer surface with a blow-torch

51

Fig. 34 Taking the solid sand candle out of the sand.

lightly. Now insert the wick in the normal way, and clean up the upper surface of the candle. Small deposits of sand on the burning surface can be removed by first melting the surface with a blowtorch, and then lifting them out with the point of a craft knife. You will almost certainly encounter shrinkage around the centre of the candle, and extra special care should be taken when topping up or melting down the surface with your blowtorch to avoid damaging the sand/wax 'rim' of the candle. The thinner it is, the more careful you must be. Finally, trim the wick, and smooth off the base of the candle so that it stands absolutely vertical.

Variations Build a solid object, such as a shell, into the basic mould shape (see illustration opposite). Use a soup-bowl for making your impression to create a fairly flat candle, and insert multiple wicks. Link several deep units with fairly narrow channels and insert a wick in each unit. Dip the finished candle in a thin layer of plain white wax for a different finish. The variations are almost infinite.

Fig. 35 A finished sand candle. For extra effect, a large shell was built into the shape of this mould, and legs, pushed through the sand with lengths of dowelling, were added.

A sand candle – second method

Equipment
Mould
Sand
Paraffin wax
Stearin
Wicking
Oil
Spatula

Fig. 36 Sand and wax mixture ready for pressing into a mould.

Fig. 37 Pressing wax and sand mixture into a small mould.

Method   Choose a mould and oil it. In another container, mix one part of wax melted to 180° F (82° C) with two parts of sand. Using a flat-bladed knife or a spatula, apply a layer of the wax/sand mixture evenly to the side and base of the mould. Leave to harden. When the mixture is fairly firm, you can embed a wick in it, and secure it at the top in the normal way. Your wax/sand shell is now ready to be filled with ordinary paraffin wax any colour you want. Pour, set, and top up in the normal way. This method of making sand candles ensures greater control of the finished outer surface of the candle, but doesn't allow the same amount of freedom of shape.

Variations   Dip the finished candle in a thin layer of plain white paraffin wax. Carve patterns out of the sand layer so that the inner wax core shows through.

Fig. 38   A small sand and wax moulded candle, dipped afterwards to give a smoother finish.

A whipped wax candle

Equipment
Mould
Paraffin wax
Stearin
Wicking
Fork or kitchen whisk

Fig. 39   Whipping some cooling wax with a rotary hand whisk.

Fig. 40   Packing the mould with whipped wax. In this case, the wick will be inserted once the mould has been packed, but *before* the wax has time to harden. It is pushed down through the centre with the point of a skewer.

Method   Prepare the mould as usual. Allow the melted
paraffin wax and stearin mixture to cool until you can whip
it with a fork or kitchen whisk. Keep whisking until the
wax looks like snow. Pack the whipped wax into a mould,
being careful to press it down firmly to avoid any air
pockets. Leave to set, and demould.

Fig. 41   The quality of candyfloss. . . . A finished whipped wax candle.

A candle in a glass

Equipment
Wax
Stearin
Wicking
Glass tumbler, brandy balloon, or other container
Skewer
Glue

Method　Take a clean, transparent glass container that is in itself attractive. Wax a length of wicking, choosing, for once, one that is slightly larger than the recommended size for the diameter of the container (this will help to keep the candle burning when the entire surface of the candle is molten: a wick that is too small could topple over and extinguish itself). Bend a short length of the wick at right angles, and glue it to the centre of the base of the glass container. Secure it at the top surface as usual. Pour melted wax (try not to exceed a temperature of 180° F (82° C) unless the glass is *very* thick) carefully and evenly into the container, and allow to set. Top up as usual, but take extra

Fig. 42　A candle in a glass. The lid which goes with this special container will protect the candle's surface from gathering dust while it is not burning, and makes it just as attractive unlit as lit.

care to achieve a smooth top surface: what would normally be the *base* of the candle is, in a candle which will not be removed from its container, the *top*. Trim the wick.

If preferred, you can insert the wick after pouring with the help of a heated skewer. Ornamental glass jars also make attractive candle containers.

These candles need no additional holders, as they will not drip.

Candles in a nutshell

Equipment
Wax
Narrow wicking
Walnuts
Craft knife

Method   With the knife, carefully halve the walnuts, and thoroughly clean out the inside of the shells. Wax the wicking, cut into one-inch (25-mm.) lengths, and bend over at right angles a short length. Glue this short length carefully to the base of the nutshell, so that the wick stands up centrally. Fill the nutshells with melted wax, but this time don't add stearin: it would shrink the wax from the side of the shells. Set, and top up.

Float the candles in a bowl of water for an unusual table centre, or use them as little floating 'boats' in your garden pond for a party.

Fig. 43   Fix the wick to the base of the shell with a dab of glue, positioning it carefully with the point of a skewer (or in this case a spatula) so that the wick, when vertical, will burn centrally.

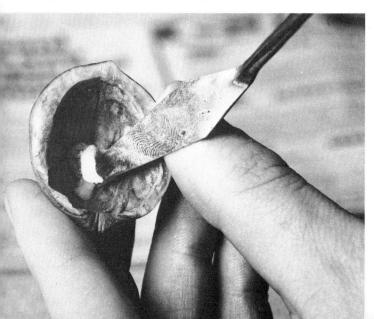

Tapers

Equipment
Length of metal rod, a strong coathanger, or wooden spoon
Paraffin wax in a wide, deep container
Water jacket
Stearin
Dye
Wicking
Sugar thermometer
Craft knife

Method Tapers are made by dipping lengths of wick into molten wax, lifting them out, letting the wax collected on the wick set, and redipping until the requisite thickness of wax is built up around the wick. A taper can be long and thin or short and fat: the only limitations on size and shape are the equipment you have at your disposal.

Everything hinges on the size and depth of container you are able to muster. If the depth of melted wax which it will comfortably hold is only six inches (15 cm.), then that is the maximum length of taper you can make. Equally, if

Fig. 44 Positioning the wicks on a coathanger.

the diameter of your container is only six inches, you won't really be able to make more than one taper at a time. Assemble your equipment, decide on its possibilities and/ or limitations, and begin by melting sufficient paraffin wax for your purpose. Cut equal lengths of wicking according to the size of taper you want, and add three inches (75 mm.) or so extra. If you are making a fat taper, remember to use a thicker wick than if you were making a thin one. Soak the wicks thoroughly in the melted paraffin wax, fish them out, and hang them up to dry as straight as possible. When they are dry, straighten out any remaining kinks, and tie them around your chosen rod (see illustration

Fig. 45 Tapers ready to light. These tapers have been made in pairs, with double lengths of wicking strung across a home-made frame.

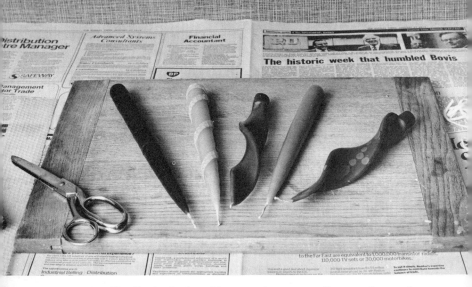

Fig. 46 A selection of home-made tapers: ordinary, undecorated tapers, a taper decorated with a swag of beeswax, and flattened, twisted tapers.

opposite) at about 2 inch (5 cm.) intervals, depending on the width of candle you intend to produce. Make sure you have a hook or hanger, away from a wall, where you can hang your tapers on their frame (if you are using a simple rod, you can suspend it across the back or seats of two chairs), and cover the surface beneath with newspaper to catch drips. Add stearin – 20 % is a good quantity – and dye, if you like, to the wax, and as soon as the temperature of the wax reaches 160° F (71° C), lift the rod carefully and, holding it absolutely horizontal, dip the suspended wicks slowly and smoothly into the wax. Hold them steady for about five seconds, and then slowly and smoothly lift them out again. Hang up the frame, and leave the tapers to dry for about two minutes. Repeat the dipping and drying process until you achieve the thickness of taper you want. Leave the finished tapers for an hour or so to set hard before you cut the tapers from the frame. Trim off the base of each one with a craft knife until it is flat.

If you enjoy making tapers, you might consider building or improvising your own frame, so that you can make several tapers at once and maximize the use to which you can put the surface area of the pot of melted wax. Short pieces of lattice fencing, wooden or metal circles, pre-cut pegboard (enlarge the holes), and many other materials make excellent taper frames.

Variations When you have built up a good thickness of wax on your wick, remove the taper from its frame, lay it

62

flat on a sheet of greaseproof paper, and roll the still pliable taper to flatten it. You can now twist this flat taper if you wish. When you are happy with the final shape, round off the base so it will fit a candle holder, and leave to harden.

A twisted taper

Equipment
Heat-resistant tin or dish
Paraffin wax
Wicking

Method Melt a quantity of wax in a shallow, heat-resistant dish or tin. Take a long length of wicking, and

Fig. 47 The ultimate in plaiting thin tapers.

pass it slowly and evenly through the melted wax. Hang up, absolutely straight, to dry. Repeat the process of drawing the wick through the wax until a taper approximately $\frac{1}{8}$ to $\frac{1}{4}$ inch (3 to 6 mm.) has been achieved. Before it is absolutely set hard, wind the taper round and round in a spiral, beginning at the base, and building up an ever-narrowing candle shape. Leave a short length of straight wicking at the top.

This is not as easy as it sounds. To build up your candle perfectly while the wax is still pliable requires speed and skill. It is advisable, therefore, before trying this technique with wax and wick, to practise the shaping of the final candle with thin 'sausages' of plasticine, until you are confident of the method.

Variations There is almost no end to the ways in which you can wind thin tapers. Study the winding of a ball of wool or string; experiment with knots; try to reproduce the shape of a banger firework; use a thicker central core, and wind thin tapers round it for purely decorative effect.

A layered multi-coloured candle

Equipment
Wax
Stearin
Wicking
Mould
Mould seal
Skewer

Method Have ready batches of differently coloured melted paraffin wax. Prepare your mould in the normal way, insert and seal the wick, and pour one 'layer' of wax into the mould to the desired depth, taking care not to splash wax onto the sides of the mould. Leave to set until a firm skin has formed, poke the surface with the skewer, and top up. Leave again until a firm skin has formed. Now pour another layer of differently coloured wax, leave to set, break the surface, top up, and continue in this way until your mould is full. Turn out the candle in the usual way.

Variations Give your candle a zigzag effect by tilting the candle on alternate sides as you pour the layers of wax (a cooling bath helps this finish). Decorate your candle.

64

Fig. 48 Bold stripes are the key to this layered candle.

A corrugated candle

Equipment
Paraffin wax
Stearin
Wicking
Wide mould
Length of corrugated cardboard

Method Line a wide mould with a strip of corrugated cardboard cut to size. Make sure that the edges of the cardboard strip are neatly butted up and tape them together. Insert the wick into the mould in the normal way. Pour wax/stearin mixture very carefully and slowly, and set and top up the candle in the normal way. Remove the candle and the cardboard together from the mould, and then firmly tear off the cardboard. Trim the wick.

Variations Traces of cardboard fibre adhering to the surface of the candle can be washed away in lukewarm water. Dip the finished candle in a hot wax bath for a smoother finish. Try using ordinary cardboard tubes instead of corrugated cardboard.

Fig. 49 A tall candle 'moulded' in corrugated cardboard.

Fig. 50   This is a real work of art. The candle itself has been painstakingly built up in layers of different-coloured wax to create the effect of a hilly landscape, and the fern leaves, carefully fixed to look like trees, have been finally anchored to the surface with a single dipped layer of white wax.

Fig. 51   Nutshells bobbing in a glass bowl.

A carved candle

Equipment
Wax
Stearin
Wide mould
Chunks of left-over wax
Wicking
Craft knife
Skewer

Method Prepare the mould and insert the wick in the normal way. Arrange chunks of wax around the wick, and fill the mould almost to overflowing. Slowly pour melted wax of a contrasting colour around the wick, filling the mould to the very top. Tap the sides of the mould gently to release air bubbles. Set and top up in the normal way. When the candle has been removed from the mould, carve away the smooth, outer layer of wax to expose the wax chunks, and create an effect like the side of a rocky mountain.

Variations Soften the finish of the candle with a blowtorch. Dip the candle in a hot wax bath.

Fig. 52 Carving out the chunks to create an effect rather like a cliff.

Fig. 53 The finished carved candle. The edges have been softened with a blowtorch.

Fig. 54 Beeswax sheets are easy to use, smell marvellous when they burn, and come in beautiful, soft colours. Honeycomb sheets are the most widely available.

Fig. 55 A well-known whisky bottle immortalized in wax.

Fig. 56 Truly straightforward paper appliqué: circular price labels are fixed to this candle to form the 'pips' of a dice.

A marbled candle

Equipment
Mould
Wax
Stearin
Small,.uneven chunks of left-over wax
Wicking
Mould seal
Skewer

Method Prepare the chosen mould and insert the wick as usual. Fill the mould with the chunks of wax, then pour melted wax of a contrasting colour slowly until the mould is full. Tap the sides of the mould gently to loosen any trapped air bubbles. Set and demould as usual.

Variations Use chunks of wax in many different colours, and fill the candle with white wax. Use different coloured layers of wax chunks, to achieve a striped effect.

Fig. 57   The mould is filled with chunks of wax of varying sizes, ready for pouring.

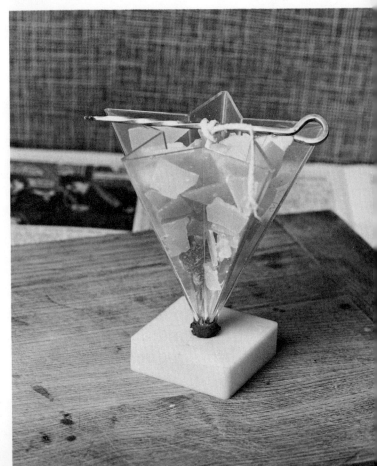

Fig. 58 A marbled candle.

Fig. 59 A lovely balloon candle, finished with bold strokes with a brush and wax. *(Below)*

Fig. 60 A delicately painted candle. Note how evenly the brushstrokes have been made. *(Right)*

Fig. 61 Fir cones embedded in a pure white candle.

A fir-cone candle

Equipment
Wax
Stearin
Wicking
Mould
Mould seal
Pine cones
Pine wax perfume

Method   Prepare the mould in the normal way, and insert and seal the wick. Arrange three or four pine cones around the base of the mould, and cover with pine-scented melted wax, white or coloured. Allow a thin skin to form, then place a further layer of pine cones on top of the wax skin. Cover with wax. Add more pine cones, and continue the process of setting the wax, positioning the pine cones, and covering with wax until the mould is full. Set and demould in the normal way.

A tinfoil candle

Equipment
Wide mould
Wicking
Paraffin wax
Stearin
Pieces of aluminium foil

Method   Prepare your candle mould as usual, and insert the wick. Now crumple pieces of aluminium foil and arrange them round the sides of the mould, making sure that at least some of the foil is actually flat against the sides of the mould. Pour the wax and set the candle as usual.

When the candle has set, dip it in a hot wax bath to coat the exposed foil with a thin layer of (preferably white) wax.

Fig. 62   Three examples of the incredible effects of swirled wax. In this case, simple tapers have been transformed into true 'special occasion' candles.

Fig. 63   Carved onion-skin surface to a candle, which has first been dipped several times to give a multi-coloured look. *(Right)*

Fig. 64   A whipped wax snowball. There is no better way of disguising a round moulded candle that has some surface fault than to cover it in a generous layer of pure white whipped wax.

Fig. 65 Tinfoil glints through the wax to add interest to a simple square candle.

A hurricane candle

Equipment
Large, wide mould of simple shape
Small glass which will fit comfortably into the mould
  without protruding at the top
Paraffin wax
Stearin
Wicking
Craft knife

Method   Find a mould large enough to hold a glass and
prepare it as usual, but seal the wick hole if there is one,
and do not insert a wick. Fill the mould with molten wax,
and allow to set until a crust about half an inch (13 mm.)
thick has formed on the top surface. Cut the top surface
away with the craft knife, leaving half an inch around the
edge, and remove the 'top' completely. Now pour out all the
liquid wax in the centre of the candle, and allow the remaining shell to harden completely. Unmould the shell, trim the
top edges, and smooth off any rough spots. Polish gently.

Prepare a candle in a glass according to the instructions on
page 58. Insert the glass carefully into the outer shell, and
position it exactly in the centre. When the inner candle
burns, the outer wax shell will glow softly. The inner
candle may be replaced indefinitely.

Variations   Decorate the outer shell by positioning leaves
or other decorations on the outside, and then fixing them
and dipping the shell in a hot wax bath. Hollow out one
or more sides of the shell, and replace the wax with tissue
paper.

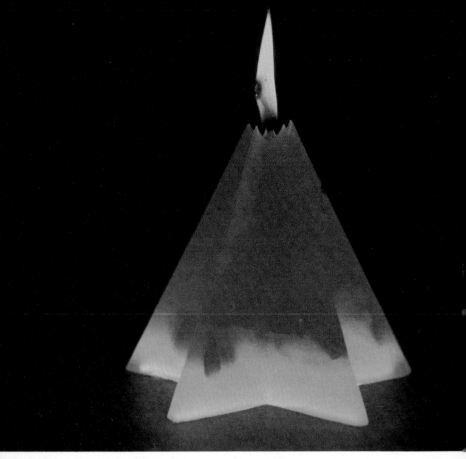

Fig. 66 A five-pointed star which combines a moulded effect with larger, unmelted chunks.

Fig. 67 Iceberg with a double wick.

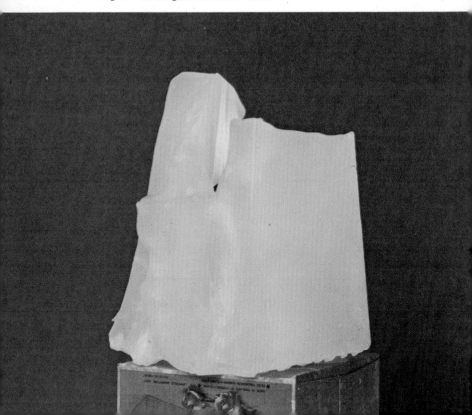

A snowman candle

Equipment
One large, round candle mould or a large cup
One medium or smaller round candle mould or a smaller
  cup
Paraffin wax
Stearin
Wicking
Flat-bladed knife
Metal skewer

Method   Using round commercial moulds or cups, mould two plain white paraffin wax spheres, though if you are using cups, you will have to mould each ball in two halves, and weld them together. Whichever method you are using, insert the wick in the smaller candle, leaving sufficient wicking hanging loose to incorporate the length of the larger candle. Now, using a hot skewer or any other drilling method, bore a wick hole through the larger ball, and insert the length of free wick attached to the small ball. Pull the wick really tight to secure the small ball – the head of the snowman – to the larger ball – his body – and seal it at the base. Using a hot knife blade or a blowtorch, weld the 'head' to the 'body'. Add cut-out paraffin wax or beeswax eyes, nose, mouth, scarf, buttons, and so on, using a sheet of half-set paraffin wax an eighth of an inch (3 mm.) thick. Fix the decorations either with simple pressure of the hand, or, for a more secure finish, with wax glue or a drop of molten wax.

Variations   Extend your snowman upwards by giving him a top hat – a small, straight-sided candle (insert the wick first in this 'hat', leaving enough spare wicking to take in the two balls for the head and body). Add a brim cut out of sheet paraffin or beeswax.

A bottle candle

Equipment
Wax
Stearin
Wicking
Beer bottle, complete with labels
Glue
Wicking needle or length of wire

Method Carefully remove the labels from your chosen bottle by soaking, and set them aside on a clean, flat surface to dry. Make sure that your bottle is completely clean and dry. Fix a swab of cotton wool to one end of your wicking needle, dip it in some glue, pass it through the neck of the bottle (taking care not to get glue on the sides of the bottle), and deposit a drop on the centre base of the bottle. Wax the wick, pass it through the wicking needle, and insert it in the bottle, affixing it carefully to the glue on the base. Leave until the glue has set, then fix the wick at the top of the bottle. Colour the melted wax as nearly as possible to the colour of your chosen bottle (or, if it's a clear bottle, of its contents), and pour, using a narrow-lipped jug, right to the bottle top. Set and top up as usual.

When the candle is completely hard, place it, in its mould, into your freezer, or the freezing compartment of your refrigerator, and chill thoroughly. Then wrap it in a rag, or an old pillowcase, and plunge it straight from the fridge into boiling water so that the glass will break. As soon as you hear or feel it cracking, remove it from the water, and release the candle from its mould.

Glue the labels you have saved in their correct positions on the bottle candle, and trim the wick.

An egg candle

Equipment
Paraffin wax
Stearin
Wicking
An egg
Skewer
Darning needle
Mould seal

Method Take an egg, and with a darning needle, pierce a tiny hole through one end of the eggshell. Make a larger hole, about half an inch (13 mm.) in diameter, in the other, by picking off bits of shell with your needle. Be careful not to crack the eggshell. Now blow or shake out the contents, and wash and dry it carefully and thoroughly. Seal the tiny hole with tape or sealant, and place the eggshell sealed end down in an eggcup. Now pour the wax smoothly into the eggshell mould, tilting it so that the sides are covered uniformly, and fill up carefully. Set in the normal way, and peel off the shell carefully. Insert the wick with great care.

Variations Scent or decorate your egg candle any way you like.

Fig. 68 A good idea for the Easter Sunday breakfast table.

Fig. 69 A balloon candle (see also *Fig. 59*).

A balloon candle

Equipment
Round balloon
Cold water
Paraffin wax
Wicking

Method   Fill a balloon with cold water, tie it, and dry it carefully. Heat the wax in a container sufficiently deep and wide to accommodate the balloon, to a temperature of about 175° F (80° C). Dip the balloon into the wax several times until a fairly thick shell of wax has formed on the surface of the balloon, allowing about thirty seconds between each dipping. When the last coat has hardened, untie the balloon very carefully, pour out the water, and lift the balloon out of the wax shell. When the shell is completely hard, you can fill it with wax at a normal pouring temperature, adding it at first in small quantities with a spoon, to be absolutely certain that the fragile wax shell will not lose its shape. The wick may be inserted into the shell before filling it up, or once the entire candle has set.

Variations   Coat the inside of the shell with swirled dye and stearin melted together, in one or more colours, before filling the candle with paraffin wax. Don't fill the shell at all, and use it as a container for a hurricane candle (see page 81).

What went wrong?

Surface faults

Lumpy surface on a dipped candle

The temperature of the dipping wax was too low. You should aim to dip your candles at a temperature of between 180° and 200° F (82° to 93° C). Try redipping at this temperature.

Misshapen rubber-moulded candle

You probably didn't support your mould well enough, or you didn't top up properly. Either way, if the candle is still pliable and can be rolled gently into shape with your hands, you may be able to save it.

Air bubbles on the surface

You didn't tap the mould to release the air after pouring – or you were just unlucky. Try melting the surface with a blowtorch, or decorating with appliqués.

A scaly surface

The pouring temperature was too low. Try dipping – but it won't work if the scaliness is really bad.

Large cracks in the surface

That you *didn't* intend! Don't cool your candle in the fridge unless you want thermal cracks – and if you *didn't* put it in the fridge, warm your room a little! Repeated dipping may conceal the faults, but if your candle is badly cracked, break it up and use it as chunks.

The candle won't leave the mould

There could be several reasons for this. You might have used insufficient stearin, you may have topped up above the original level, or you may have cooled the mould too slowly. Whatever the reason, the only remedy is to put the mould in hot water, and melt the candle out.

The colours on layered candles seem to have merged

This is a sure sign that you were in too much of a hurry to pour the different layers. If the surface of the previous layer is not sufficiently set, it will remelt when you pour more hot wax on top of it, and the colours will merge. You can only learn the right time to pour the next layer from experience. So count this candle as an experimental one and break it into chunks. (Don't forget that if you melt several colours together, the result will be muddy brown!)

The colours on a layered candle aren't joined

This time, you waited too long between pouring the layers – and you *didn't* pierce each layer around the centre as an 'anchor'. Alternatively, the wax wasn't hot enough. Either way, unless the colours are strong enough to withstand repeated dipping, break the candle up into chunks.

A small bubbly line encircles the candle

This is caused by using a cooling bath whose depth is lower than the level of wax in the mould. You could decorate to conceal this fault.

Small pitmarks on the surface

Again, this is usually associated with using a cooling bath, if you plunge the candle into it immediately after pouring. You *must* allow the air bubbles to settle before putting the mould in the bath. Alternative reasons might be that you poured the wax too hot, or too quickly (thereby trapping more air bubbles).

Vertical scratches on the candle

This is most likely to happen with home-made moulds, though it may be encountered with some commercial ones. It means generally that the inner edge of the mould is not completely smooth. Check the mould carefully, and sand down any rough edges with emery paper to avoid future disasters. If you have a metal mould, you have probably dented the edge. Try straightening it out, but resign yourself to throwing away the mould completely if this doesn't work. If you have metal cutting tools, you may be able to cut the edge down to remove the offending dent – but if you are inexperienced in these matters, take great care of flying metal shavings. Decorate the scratched surface, or remelt the candle.

Mottled appearance

The candle has probably been cooled too slowly – and maybe you didn't add enough stearin. Try repeated dipping, or remelt the candle.

The sides of the candle have caved in

If this seems to have happened when you remove your candle from its mould, there's no remedy – just remelt. You probably didn't poke holes in the half-set surface for topping up.

Burning faults

The candle smokes badly

Most probably the wick you have used is too large – but you could also have added too little stearin to the wax.

The flame is too small

If this is the case, then your wick is probably too small. But you may have added too much stearin to the wax, thereby making it more difficult to burn.

The candle drips – unintentionally

Wick size, again, may be the problem here. If the wick is too large, it will melt too large a surface area, and cause dripping. If the wick is too small, it won't be able to consume all the melted wax – and that will probably drip over the edge. If the dripping is only on one side of the candle, it is probably not completely vertical, so check that the base is flat on the holder, and that the candle itself wasn't made at an angle (use a plumb line). If the candle does slant, shave away the base until you have corrected the fault.

The candle spits when it burns

Somehow you've managed to get water into the candle. Try pouring away the molten wax around the wick, and relighting. If this doesn't work, remelt the candle.

The candle keeps going out

Again, your wick is too small. A vast sea of molten wax around a thin wick only encourages the wick to topple and extinguish itself.

The wick in a beautiful sand candle has burned right down

The basic problem is, of course, that the wick's too small. But with 'container' candles you can always replace the wick, and top up the candle again and again. You can even change the colour of the wax if you are careful to carve away the remains of the previous colour in a sand candle.

Decorating your candles

The simple, basic shape of a candle is in itself sufficiently beautiful; but there are occasions when you will want to change or augment this shape – to emphasize colour, for a special occasion, or because the finish on your candle is in some way damaged. You shouldn't embellish a candle just for the sake of it: a simple, uncluttered shape combined with attractive colouring can be completely ruined by fussy decoration.

This said, there are a number of ways in which you can use surface decoration to enhance your candles. This section outlines the basic techniques – but, once again, the methods listed are only intended as catalysts for your own imagination. The scope is infinite.

Carving

A craft knife, with a selection of different blades, is an excellent tool for decoration. Carving candles is a skilled operation, however, and the inexperienced candlemaker should not embark upon ambitious patterns without a few test runs on old candles or an unmelted block of wax.

Circular holes of varying depths and diameters carved out of the surface of a large candle look very attractive, and are fairly easy for the beginner. So are simple shapes, traced from pictures, and transferred to the candle surface ready for carving: Christmas trees, simple flower patterns, figures (for birthday candles), or words (names, for example). If you are good at whittling or woodcarving, decorating a candle in this way will be no problem.

Carved candles look better buffed up with a soft cloth to even off the rough edges.

Cutting back a sand-moulded candle

Interesting and attractive effects can be created on a sand-moulded candle if the outer sand and wax casing is cut

Fig. 70 This candle has not been carved by hand, but by using a wood-worker's lathe. Simplicity is the keynote: the two carved grooves are perfectly balanced. One more, or one less, would have spoiled the effect.

back in places to reveal the wax centre. As the candle burns, the light will glow through at the points where the outer casing has been cut back.

Circles and squares are the easiest shapes to try to cut out, especially if the candle has a thick sand and wax shell.

Fig. 71 Cutting back a thickly moulded sand candle until pure wax shows through. When the candle burns, this will glow beautifully.

Fig. 72 Even, regular strokes with the head of a hammer will give this kind of finish to your candle.

Surface grooves

Use a heated skewer, or a long nail (minus its head) driven into a wooden handle, or a soldering iron to make linear grooves in the surface of your candle. The secret is to apply even pressure on your chosen tool, and to draw it across or down the surface of the candle at an absolutely even rate. Move too fast, and you won't make sufficient impression on the surface. Move too slowly, and you may cause drips or blobs that look unsightly. Experiment first with an old candle, or on a block of solid wax, before starting work on your candle.

To make circular indentations in the surface, try heating the head of a nail and driving it into the candle surface. Any metal shape which will conduct heat and which, of

Fig. 73   Using a large nail head to make impressions on the surface of a candle.

course, you can *hold* can be used to pattern the surface in this way. Modernistic and exciting surface patterns can be created with nuts and bolts, precast metal components for machines, and other utilitarian objects.

Hammering

Larger candles look good with a hammered surface. You can use any solid object as a hammer – a block of wood, the handle of a spoon, a spanner, or a hammer itself. Simply hit the surface of the candle firmly but with even pressure, either in a random pattern or in a preselected line. (You can safely outline your pattern with the tip of your craft knife before beginning to hammer it.)

Hammering a dipped candle while its surface is still pliable will create a soft effect. Hammering on a completely hard candle surface will give a bolder, more angular effect.

This technique is particularly useful for 'saving' candles with a damaged surface. It is easiest to apply to simple, moulded candles rather than uneven, free-form ones.

Spanking

Using a wire brush with fairly long 'bristles', you can spank the surface of the candle to produce an attractive frosted effect.

Painting with poster paints

Relief candles made in commercial rubber moulds cry out for a touch of paint to highlight the surface design. Poster paints are ideal for this job, and you can buy these from any artists' supplier.

Painting relief mouldings requires little or no artistic talent; but if you are a keen painter as well as a candle-maker, a candle can provide an excellent canvas for creative work with poster paint.

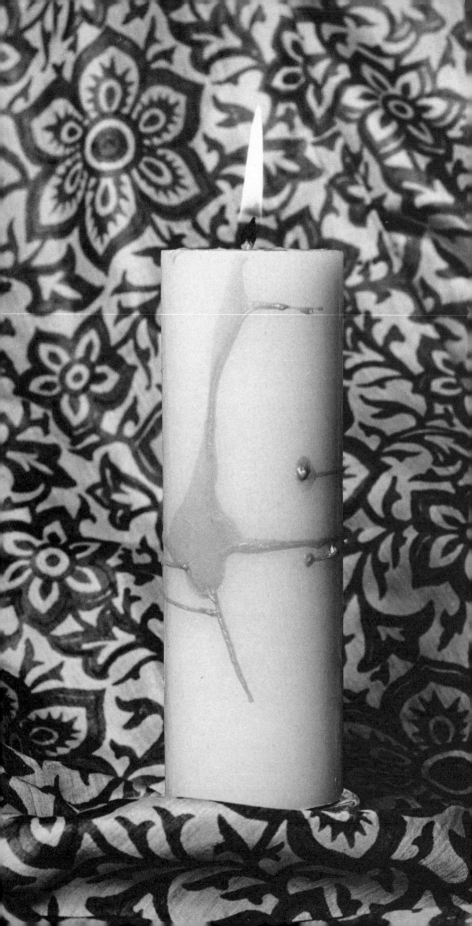

Painting with wax

Using an ordinary artists' watercolour brush and a little hot coloured wax, candles can be decorated in much the same way as with poster paints. Wax, however, solidifies quickly, so speed and simplicity of line are essential. You will need a different brush for each colour you are using. Afterwards, soak the brushes in hot water, and make certain they are absolutely dry before using them again.

A fine paint-brush and melted wax can also be used to build up polka dot patterns – drip the wax from the tip of the brush onto the candle, and leave to set. You can combine brushwork, too, with other kinds of decoration.

Dipping

The technique involved in making tapers (see page 60) can be used in many ways in the decoration of a finished candle. If you intend to dip your finished candle, leave an extra long length of wick on it, so that you can hold the candle firmly while doing so.

A dipped candle, particularly when ordinary white paraffin wax has been used, looks softer and less angular than an undipped candle. Therefore, dip candles which have surface pits or scrapes, either in the same colour as the candle itself if surface damage is bad, or in a different colour. An interesting and attractive effect is created by repeatedly dipping a candle in melted wax of a contrasting colour, letting it set hard, and then carving out sections to show the colour of the original candle. You can repeat this process with as many different colours of wax as you wish.

Dipping can also be used as an attractive way of anchoring surface appliqués. Paper cut-outs, leaves, wax appliqués etc. can all be encased in a thin layer of white wax for a more permanent and softer effect.

Fig. 74   No actual 'wax' was used for this 'painted' effect: stearin and dye, melted together, were dripped on to the surface of the candle, and then moved around until a pattern formed. The colour is intense and arresting.

Dripping

Many people like the effect of dripping wax on the surface of a candle. Nearly every candle will develop its own drip pattern as it burns, but you can make drips of wax part of the original decoration of your candle. You will need a blowtorch, a bunsen burner, or some other source of a naked flame such as a gas poker. A blowtorch is easiest and most effective.

Using a low flame, begin to melt the wax round the top of the candle, but don't melt the wick surface itself. Keep the candle vertical. As the wax melts, it will run down the sides of the candle in the same way as it would during the course of burning. You can also trickle a very little dye and stearin, mixed and melted, onto the surface as it melts to create a multicoloured cascade of drips. The more wax you melt from the sides of the candle, the chunkier the effect of the dripping becomes.

Be bold with this technique: a few thin trickles of melted wax down the sides of the candle look like a mistake rather than decoration!

Nail varnish

Nail varnish painted evenly over the surface of a candle gives an interesting lacquered finish, and can be used in place of glue or melted wax to anchor other surface appliqués.

Whipped wax

Whipped wax has something of the quality of snow or candy floss about it: it makes an ideal decoration for a round candle which you would like to turn into a snowball, if you use plain white wax, or for a very soft and feminine candle in pale pastel colours.

The technique involves cooling melted wax, coloured if desired, until it can be whipped up into a light, creamy, fairly solid mass with a fork or a rotary whisk. The whipped wax is then applied with a spatula or a broad-bladed knife to the surface of a candle.

100

Whipped wax looks much better covering the entire candle than applied to sections or in blobs, though the choice is yours. Remember, however, that if you *are* covering your candle completely, you will have to leave an extra length of wick on the top surface so that the wick still protrudes through the whipped wax.

Fig. 75 Enforced 'dripping' using a blowtorch. It's fun to do, and the larger the dripped layers, the more interesting the candle!

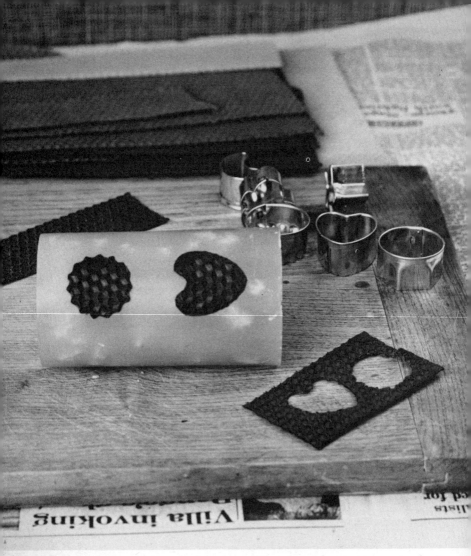

Fig. 76 Positioned appliqués cut from a sheet of beeswax.

Beeswax appliqué

Beeswax sheeting can be cut easily with a craft knife or scissors into motifs for appliqué work. There's no need to keep the ready-cut motifs in hot water prior to application.

Beeswax can also be cut into strips and plaited, and used as a complete outer facing for a candle with a disappointing finish.

Swirled wax

The swirled wax technique is a marvellous way of trans-forming a plain cylindrical candle into something really special. Take a flat-based dish approximately one to two inches (25 to 50 mm.) wider than your candle, and cover it inside and out with foil. A dessert plate, or even a round pie dish, is fine. Pour a layer of wax (it looks better if the colour is the same as the colour of the candle) into the dish. This wax will form the base of the candle, so the depth depends very much on the height and weight of the candle you are decorating. Place the candle in the centre, and allow the melted wax to harden round it.

Fill a plastic bucket or other deep container with cold water. Now pour an additional quantity of melted wax, at about 165° F (74° C) into the bowl containing the candle. Holding the candle firmly around its top surface, lower it on to the surface of the water in the bucket until the water is lapping around the edge of the bowl. Now firmly plunge the candle into the water, rotating it slowly. The newly-poured wax will set, and adhere in wispy swathes to the sides of the candle.

Paraffin wax appliqué

Pour melted wax into a toffee tray or shallow baking tray, so that a thin sheet of wax forms. Allow to set, but not hard. Now cut shapes with your craft knife, freehand, out of the sheet, or use pastry or tiny candy cutters to stamp out decorative motifs. If the wax shows signs of hardening before you have finished, place the baking tray over a dish of boiling water.

Float the motifs in a bowl of hot water to keep them pliable until you are ready to fix them to your candle.

Fixing can be done with glue, with melted wax, or by bonding the edges of the motif to the candle with the care-ful use of a soldering iron or heated skewer.

103

The motifs can themselves be decorated (for example, by pressing pencil points into them), and a relief effect can be built up by using two or more motifs on top of each other. As usual, the candle can be dipped afterwards.

Fig. 77   Tiny candy moulds, or moulds for making cocktail canapés, are ideal for cutting appliqué shapes from a thin layer of paraffin wax. Keep them soft and pliable in a bowl of hot water. Here an appliqué is being 'soldered' to the candle: in this case, with the heated point of a wicking needle.

Fig. 78 The finished effect.

Wax flower appliqués

Make one or more flower candles, of a size suitable to the candle you plan to decorate, according to the instructions on pages 42 and 44, but omit the central candle and wick. Fix these to the candle with glue, or with a little melted wax.

Fig. 79 An oblong candle (from a home-made paper mould) enhanced by a paraffin wax flower.

Fig. 80   This candle shows wax chunks, fixed to the surface, and dipped and redipped until a fairly smooth surface results.

Wax chunks as appliqué

Break up into small pieces some left-over chunks of wax, either in a complementary colour to that of the candle to be decorated, or in several colours. Cover the surface of the candle with a generous layer of wax glue, and press on the chunks. Shake off small, loose pieces when the glue has set. Dip the candle in white wax: the chunks will melt slightly to give a marbled effect.

Sand and wax appliqué

Mix two parts of wax melted to 180° F (82° C) with one part of sand. Using a flat-bladed knife or spatula, apply this to the surface of the candle in a decorative way. Sand ridges running vertically down the length of a long, fairly thin candle are most attractive. You can apply sand and wax to carved patterns and heat-impressed circles or squares for an unusual effect.

Paper appliqué

Christmas card illustrations, pictures from well-printed magazines, or even just home-made paper shapes can make attractive appliqués. Fix them with glue, and dip the candle so that the finish is preserved.

The small, adhesive price labels used by supermarkets are also good for paper appliqué work. Use several labels overlapping to build up patterns, or place small, circular labels on a square candle to turn it into a dice.

Appliqué with leaves and petals

Natural materials make delightful appliqués. Position them firmly with glue, and then dip the candle.

Moulded appliqués

Most craft suppliers stock plastic or rubber two-part moulds for use in plaster modelling. They are fine for candlemaking too. Simply pour hot wax into the mould, allow to set, and fix the moulded shape to your candle.

Linocut motifs

You can repeat a decorative motif by making a linocut, and then pressing softened wax into the linoleum where it has been cut away. The resulting impression on the wax is fairly deep and precise.

Modelling wax is easiest to use in this way, but beeswax and paraffin wax are fine if kept soft in hot water.

Plaster of Paris, wood, or soap can also be carved to form useful appliqué moulds. Plaster or wood give the most definite 'lines' to your appliqués.

Stencils

You can buy a great variety of stencils from your art shop, or make them yourself with card and scissors or a sharp knife. A stencil is easier to apply to a square or oblong candle rather than to a round one – for obvious reasons. Hold the stencil firmly against the surface to be decorated, and paint the exposed surface with wax. Then dab on a thin layer of glue and apply glitter or tiny flakes of wax – or use any decorating method you wish.

Be careful to lift the stencil off the surface firmly and in one stroke, so as not to damage the edge of your design.

Modelling wax

Your supplier will almost certainly sell modelling wax – an especially formulated wax with a very low melting point, which becomes soft and pliable when handled. It is ideal for wax appliqué work, and much easier to handle than either straightforward paraffin wax or beeswax.

With modelling wax you can perform any of the decorating exercises suggested here for paraffin wax and beeswax – and more. You can work in much more detail with modelling wax; roll it into thin sausages and press it onto the candle's surface; roll it into tiny balls and build up a relief pattern with them; make beautiful flowers; sculpt figures and faces freehand. . . . The possibilities are endless.

Everlasting flowers

Everlasting flowers, which you can purchase from a florist, make really attractive appliqués. Push a small-headed, short pin through the centre of each flower head, and then into the candle.

To soften the finished effect, and make the flowers look as if they belonged to the candle, you can either dip the flowers in white wax prior to fixing them on to the candle, or dip the candle once the flowers have been fixed (though beware of drips).

Fig. 81 Pinning everlasting flowers to a beeswax taper.

Fig. 82   A beeswax taper enhanced with pinned everlasting flowers, each of which was individually dipped in white wax before positioning.

Transfers

You can buy a wide range of decorative transfers from your supplier. They are simply applied, but you should polish the surface of the candle to a smooth finish with a soft cloth first. Once the transfer is fixed, you can dip the candle in white wax to completely seal in the transfer, and to give a softer effect.

Glitter

For a frosted effect, you can dust glitter on to whipped wax before it has set, or direct on to a candle surface that has been coated with a thin layer of glue.

Sequins

Sequins can be used to create glamorous shimmering effects. Glue them to your candle if you are making a fairly 'open' pattern, but use tiny pins if you want a lot of them.

Sea shells

Sea shells make attractive appliqués. Used around the base of a candle in conjunction with sand and wax, you can create a stunning table centrepiece.

Christmas cracker decorations

Glued or pinned to a candle, Christmas cracker decorations are an instant way of making a plain candle look festive.

Fig. 83 Ready for the festive season: a gay candle, decorated with the appliqués saved from last year's Christmas crackers.

Advanced equipment

Life can be a lot easier for the candlemaker with a few special tools to hand. But there is neither any need, nor any point, for the beginner to put together a range of special candlemaking tools. There are plenty of things around the home to satisfy most people's needs.

Start looking in the kitchen for objects you can use for hammering (the handle of a spoon, a steel for sharpening carving knives, a toffee hammer), for moulding (cups, glasses, patty tins, ice cube makers, empty cans and cartons), and for welding (flat-bladed knives, spatulas, salamanders). The household toolkit, too, is a huge source of items for decoration and finishing: hammers, chisels, nuts and bolts, cutting tools, files, and so on.

If you are a woodworker as well as a candlemaker, try using the tools for the former for making candles. Remember that wax is a softer medium than wood, and use your machinery at a low speed and with care. Clean up machinery carefully after use, as wax will clog moving parts. Remember, too, to buffer your candle from any retaining pins or clamps with a wad of cotton wool or newspaper so as to avoid surface damage.

Most homes have a soldering-iron around somewhere. Even if it does not have a detachable bit, it is still useful for small welding jobs such as wax appliqué work, and for making melted grooves in a candle's surface. If you buy a soldering-iron with a detachable bit, you can make for it any number of differently shaped tools for use in a variety of ways. Your local plumber or electrician would probably make things to your requirements, and advise you on the best materials. I find a short metal knife (preferably copper, and definitely not steel), about two inches (50 mm.) long and a quarter of an inch (6 mm.) thick, welded or screwed to the basic bit, an excellent carving tool, and useful, too, for small welding jobs. Two ordinary bits, welded together to form an 'o' in section, make an excellent tool for decoration. Longer, shorter, fancier adaptations of the soldering iron bit can be made

114

to your requirements, but remember that the longer the bit, the lower the heat that will reach its tip, and the slower the work with it.

Most homes today have an electric drill, too, and this is another invaluable tool for the candlemaker. You can replace the short standard drill bit with one sufficiently long to drill right through the length of a candle to make a wick hole quickly and accurately. A length cut from an ordinary wire coathanger, filed at one end to a pencil point, is fine, or you can buy a length of hardened steel for greater durability. For drilling work with an extra long bit, take great care to use the lowest possible speed. Your bit may bend at high speeds, and may not drill a straight, accurate path. High-speed pressure on the candle, too, could cause it to split, so work in short bursts and clean out loose wax from the drilled hole regularly. Never apply more pressure to the bit than is absolutely necessary to keep it steady.

Those wire brush attachments you can buy for an electric drill give an interesting finish to a candle – but don't expect to be able to use the brush for anything else afterwards, as you'll never be able to remove the wax from the bristles. It's easier and safer to move the candle around when working with this drill attachment than to move the drill, so work with the drill in a commercial stand. You can cover the brush with layers of newspaper and a final thick layer of soft cloth or chamois leather for speedy polishing, buffing up, or 'smoothing off' sharp carvings; you can soak a soft cloth in poster paint, cover the brush head with the cloth, and apply your colour with the revolving brush head for a new effect. In fact, with an electric drill, a few basic commercial attachments, and imagination, you can create really excitingly individual candlemaking effects, and save yourself a lot of time on basics.

If you are keen on making free-form candles and find cutting and especially welding large wax blocks a long-winded procedure, a hot wire welder/cutter would be a useful tool. Don't try making one yourself, unless you are a qualified electrician. You will need a small transformer, 3 to 4 volts output maximum, mains input, and capable of delivering at least 5 amps. This can be bought from an electronics shop. Get an electrician to connect this up for you to two copper rods (or two metal file handles), joined by a length of copper wire (if the tool is for cutting) or resistance tape (if the tool is for welding). All *you* do is to hold the wire taut, and pull it through the wax block where the cut, or the weld, is to be made. For cutting wax blocks, it is useful to have a second pair of hands to keep the blocks apart after the wire has cut them. They'll re-weld if left to themselves.

A final word: if your electrician really *is* friendly, and you've a particular problem you think he may be able to solve, explain your difficulty, and see if he can come up with a special tool for the purpose. He probably can.

Candle holders

The purpose of a candle holder is first and foremost functional – to catch the inevitable drips, and to protect your furniture and linen. If a holder does not do this, it's worthless. That said, however, there is little point in slaving over a hot mould if your finished candle is going to recline in a holder that is either intrinsically ugly or in some way conflicts with the candle itself – in shape, in colour or in style. A heavily-decorated candle will look silly sitting atop a thin, ultra-modern stem; and a plain taper looks even less at home in a heavy, highly ornate container. Good sense and good taste are at the heart of choosing the right holder for your finished candle.

Your local junk shop is a rich source of reclaimable brass candlesticks. Broken candlesticks can be stuck together again (be sure to take advice on how to do this – metal isn't always easy to re-weld), and, if they have a jolly, rounded shape, can be painted in a glossy, bright colour that fits in with your décor. Also, your supplier will stock a good range of traditional and modern holders, spanning the whole range of candle sizes. Nowadays, using candles in the home is not just confined to the romantic dinner party or the power cut, and beautiful hanging holders and permanent wall fixtures in wood and metal are now available. They are an excellent idea – particularly if there are children in your home – as they allow you to burn your candles safely, without fear of knocking them over.

Of course, if you are a woodcarver, a sculptor or a do-it-yourselfer, you can make your own candle holders. Materials from plastics to attractive pieces of wood, stone or metal picked up on a country walk make marvellous starting points.

For a special occasion, or if you want to display a brand new candle but haven't a suitable holder to hand, improvise your own with a china bowl or plate. Fix the candle firmly to the centre base with a little melted wax, and fill the bowl with objects that reflect the spirit of the candle – fresh, dried or artificial flowers (not paper), seashells,

Fig. 84 A selection of modern candle holders.

sand, coloured marbles, or even aluminium foil or
Christmas tree decorations. For a table centre for a large
dinner, use four or more identical candles on a large plate,
suitably decorated.

Finally, a word on using candle holders. Always make certain your candle is right in the middle, and absolutely vertical, or you run the risk of uneven burning and lopsidedness as the candle burns. Try to position it away from draughts, which can also affect the even burning of a lighted candle.

Make your candles pay

It's fun to make candles for yourself, to experiment with new techniques, and to make candles for friends' birthdays and so on. But sooner or later, if you really enjoy candle-making, you'll run out of people to give your candles to. Now's the time to think about selling them. You'll know yourself which types of candle you are best at making, but are they the ones that will sell? You may think you know, but just check by showing your friends a selection, and asking them to pick out the ones they like best. You may get some surprises.

Having chosen the designs you want to sell, make up a few in different colours. Work out what it cost you to make them. Bearing this figure in mind, walk round your local candle shop or department store and take a look at the prices they are charging for candles of a similar size and style. Normally, the retail price will be about 50% more than they paid for the candle. Work out this figure: would *you* make a profit if you sold to them at that price? Would it be a worthwhile profit? If it wouldn't, how much more could you safely ask?

Once you've made up your mind on a price, take along some candles, carefully wrapped, to show to the buyer. They're busy people, so don't waste time beating about the bush. If your candles are accepted for sale, even if it's only on a sale or return basis, you're in business.

Once you're established with one supplier, you have a choice: either to mass-produce, or to remain a home crafts-man making individual candles for sale at a high price. The decision is up to you. Choose the latter and your candlemaking activities won't tax you much more than a hobby – it's up to you to make what you want, when you want. You will probably, in the long run, cover the costs of your candlemaking materials, but make very little pro-fit. Decide to mass-produce, and you're letting yourself in for real business. You will need to buy (and store) materials in bulk, increase your working space to accom-modate more moulds, and invest in larger melting pots and other equipment. It also means getting used to the idea of making candles to a deadline. Finally, you'll have to start thinking about the best way to package and deliver, and work out real price scales based on large quantities. This way, you'll make more money – but you may lose out on satisfaction.

At the present, candle shops and candlemakers' suppliers are springing up just about everywhere. Candles are an expanding market, whether you mean to stay small, or get big, so there's plenty of room for good candlemakers, and plenty of people who want to buy their products.

Suppliers

Those who operate a mail-order service are marked with an asterisk.

Great Britain

For more local information on suppliers, see the *Studio Vista Guide to Craft Suppliers of Great Britain* by Judy Allen.

Candle Makers Supplies*, 4 Beaconsfield Terrace Road, London W14 0PP

The Candles Shop*, 89 Parkway, London NW1

The Candles Shop*, 9 The Broadway, White Hart Lane, London SW13

Carberry Candles*, Carberry, Musselburgh, Midlothian EH21 8P2

Celmi Candles, Cynfal House, Ffestiniog, Merioneth

Craftco*, 30 Prince of Wales Crescent, London NW1

Craft O'Hans*, The Hobby Horse, New Ash Green, Nanmerch, Flintshire

USA

Pourette Manufacturing Co.*, 8818 Roosevelt Way, N.E. Seattle, Washington 98115

American Handicrafts Co.*, 18–20 West 14th Street, New York (and many branches)

Ross Wax Company, 6–10 Ash Street, Jersey City, New Jersey 07304

Candlelite House*, 4228 East Easter Place, Littleton, Colorado 80120

Wicks and Wax Candle Shop*, 350 North Atlantic Avenue, Cocoa Beach, Florida 32931

Canada

Lumi-Craft (Canada) Ltd*, PO Box 666, Kingston, Ontario

South Africa

Camp-O-Matic Ltd*, PO Box 21, Lansdowne, Capetown

Bibliography

Carey, Mary *Candlemaking* Evans, London 1974

Collins, Paul *Introducing Candlemaking* Batsford, London 1972

Leinwoll, Stanley *Candles and Candlecrafting* Scribners, New York 1973

Leisure Crafts *Candle Making* Search Press, London 1971 and Herder and Herder, New York 1971

McLaughlin, Terence *Candle Making* Pelham Books, London 1973

Monroe, Ruth *Kitchen Candlecrafting* Yoseloff, London 1970 and A. S. Barnes, New Jersey 1970

Newman, Thelma R. *Creative Candlemaking* Allen and Unwin, London 1972

Schutz, Walter E. *Getting Started in Candlemaking* Bruce Publishing Co., London 1972 and Collier Books, New York 1972

Strose, Susanne *Candle-Making* Oak Tree Press, London 1969 and Sterling Publishing Co., New York 1972

Unger, Joan Ann *Creative Candlecraft* Grosset and Dunlap, New York 1972

Index

Figures in bold type refer to illustration numbers, and not to page numbers.

126